Preparing for Jesus

AN ADVENT DEVOTIONAL

Internet addresses given in this book were accurate at the time it went to press.

Printed in the United States of America

Published in Hellertown, PA

Cover and interior illustrations by Angela Filer

Library of Congress Control Number 2022907875

ISBN 978-1-952481-93-2

2 4 6 8 10 9 7 5 3 1

For more information or to place bulk orders, contact the publisher at Jennifer@BrightCommunications.net.

Bright
COMMUNICATIONS

BrightCommunications.net

*To Blaik, Stew, Scott, and Jeff for being faithful
pastors and cherished friends on my faith journey*

CONTENTS

INTRODUCTION

Every year, as we approach Christmas, our churches break out the annual Advent lessons. We light candles as we recite the words of hope shared by Old Testament prophets such as Micah and Isaiah. Our sermons center on angelic visitors with big news. And our Sunday school children diligently prepare to reenact the trip to Bethlehem that culminates in Jesus' arrival.

Every year, it seems, we skip over the first 17 verses of Matthew's gospel. Sometimes we acknowledge Jesus' genealogy (as long as we don't have to read the names aloud). We connect the dots from Abraham through David to Jesus, but we do little else with this portion of the text. I had been attending church for 40 years when I first heard a sermon on the genealogy of Jesus— and that was *after* this book was more than halfway completed.

This is not a criticism. To be fair, Advent Sundays are at a premium—we only get four each year. And since narratives and prophecies preach better, Jesus' genealogy seldom makes the final cut.

Yet, Matthew began his account of Jesus' life with a genealogy for a reason. He detailed the road from Abraham to Jesus for a purpose. In search of that purpose, I visited each available stop on that road, asking at every checkpoint, "What does this have to do with Jesus?"

I discovered on this journey that each of Jesus' ancestors prepares us for Jesus' arrival in his or her own unique way. Some stories reveal our need for a savior, while others illustrate a hope or a promise. But all of them enrich our understanding of who Jesus is, what he has done for us, and why it matters.

The book in your hands is my takeaway from that journey. Exploring the stories of Jesus' human ancestors has provided me an opportunity to visit portions of the Bible that are less familiar and less talked about, and that has been a transformative experience. My prayer is, as you spend the next 28 days retracing this journey through Jesus' lineage that you, too, will be enriched and challenged by these passages and prepared to receive Jesus more fully and completely than ever.

In His peace,
Jac

HOW TO USE THIS BOOK

Like other devotionals, this book is portioned into small daily readings. Because this is an Advent devotional, we explore each of the daily readings through the familiar lens of the Christmas story.

Also, like other devotionals, you will be invited to reflect on the material and guided to pray over it as you apply the lessons of the passage to your life and circumstance.

Unlike other devotionals, you will be guided to read more than a single verse or paragraph of scripture. Instead, each day's reading will direct you to a passage (or passages) that relay a whole scene. This is by design.

You might read as few as nine verses one day or up to 30 another day, but each reading will take you only a few minutes. The Bible tells its story better than I can, so I have aimed to make my words few, to serve only as a guide as the rich narratives of scripture speak for themselves.

THE GENEALOGY OF
JESUS THE MESSIAH

[1] This is the genealogy[a] of Jesus the Messiah[b] the son of David, the son of Abraham:

[2] Abraham was the father of Isaac,

Isaac the father of Jacob,

Jacob the father of Judah and his brothers,

[3] Judah the father of Perez and Zerah, whose mother was Tamar,

Perez the father of Hezron,

Hezron the father of Ram,

[4] Ram the father of Amminadab,

Amminadab the father of Nahshon,

Nahshon the father of Salmon,

[5] Salmon the father of Boaz, whose mother was Rahab,

Boaz the father of Obed, whose mother was Ruth,

Obed the father of Jesse,

[6] and Jesse the father of King David.

David was the father of Solomon, whose mother had been Uriah's wife,

[7] Solomon the father of Rehoboam,

Rehoboam the father of Abijah,

Abijah the father of Asa,

⁸ Asa the father of Jehoshaphat,

Jehoshaphat the father of Jehoram,

Jehoram the father of Uzziah,

⁹ Uzziah the father of Jotham,

Jotham the father of Ahaz,

Ahaz the father of Hezekiah,

¹⁰ Hezekiah the father of Manasseh,

Manasseh the father of Amon,

Amon the father of Josiah,

¹¹ and Josiah the father of Jeconiah[c] and his brothers at the time of the exile to Babylon.

¹² After the exile to Babylon:

Jeconiah was the father of Shealtiel,

Shealtiel the father of Zerubbabel,

¹³ Zerubbabel the father of Abihud,

Abihud the father of Eliakim,

Eliakim the father of Azor,

¹⁴ Azor the father of Zadok,

Zadok the father of Akim,

Akim the father of Elihud,

¹⁵ Elihud the father of Eleazar,

Eleazar the father of Matthan,

Matthan the father of Jacob,

[16] and Jacob the father of Joseph, the husband of Mary, and Mary was the mother of Jesus who is called the Messiah.

[17] Thus there were fourteen generations in all from Abraham to David, fourteen from David to the exile to Babylon, and fourteen from the exile to the Messiah.

—Matthew 1:1-17

FOOTNOTES

a. Matthew 1:1 Or *is an account of the origin*

b. Matthew 1:1 Or *Jesus Christ. Messiah* (Hebrew) and *Christ* (Greek) both mean *Anointed One*; also in verse 18.

c. Matthew 1:11 That is, Jehoiachin; also in verse 12

Day 1

ABRAHAM: PREPARING FOR A NEW START

READ: *Genesis 12:1–9*

For us, Christmas comes every year. And every year, we go into the same storage area and pull out the same decorations that we had used the past year. We get together with the same family, and we eat much of the same food. We seldom have a reason to associate the word "new" with Christmas. But as we look at the story of Abraham, we are reminded just how new Jesus' arrival really was.

Before Abraham, the world had experienced two large scale divine responses to human sin. First, a flood, from which only Noah and his family were spared. Second, the dispersion of the people from Babel, both geographically and linguistically. And now, God was initiating a new response to human sin, one that would culminate in forgiveness and redemption.

Abraham's call was unprecedented. The plan that God was launching was so new and so different that He required Abraham to walk away from all that was familiar. Abraham left behind his family as well as his security, inheritance, and the legacy of his first 75 years of life to be a part of God's redemption plan. And that plan would reach its fullness with something equally new and unprecedented: God taking on flesh and dwelling among us.

REFLECT: In Jesus we are made new, and by the Holy Spirit, we are continually renewed. In what ways has God called you to live in newness for Him? Have you been called to mission, a new job, a new city, or simply new activities and priorities?

 PRAY: Take some time to thank God for all of the ways that He has made you new. Ask Him to show you where He is growing, shaping, and calling you into further newness.

Day 2

ABRAHAM: PREPARING TO BELIEVE

READ: *Genesis 15:1–6, James 2:20–24, Genesis 22:15–18*

As children, many of us believed in Santa Claus. And we acted on our belief, by working hard to stay on the "nice" list, sending letters to the North Pole, and putting out cookies on Christmas Eve. But as we matured, we rightly shed our belief in Santa Claus.

By contrast, when we mature as Christians, our belief increases because we have experienced God's faithfulness. God calls us to believe Jesus' miraculous birth, his identity, and his purpose. And God calls us to put our belief into action, much the way we did as children anticipating Santa's arrival and much the way Abraham did when he was given an extraordinary promise by God.

Abraham was already an old man when God set him on a new path and promised him a lasting legacy of uncountable offspring. Despite Abraham's old age and lack of children, he believed, and eventually Isaac was born.

Even when Abraham's faith was tested, and he was asked to surrender to God the very son that was promised him, his belief in God's promise did not waver. Just as Isaac's promised arrival defied logic, God's request that Abraham return Isaac to him defied human understanding, yet Abraham chose to believe, trust, and obey. Then God responded to Abraham's faith by rescuing Isaac and by affirming His promise again to Abraham.

REFLECT: In the Christmas story, we find that there is much that we believe on faith, including the virgin birth, the angelic announcement, the star, and—most of all—that Jesus is Emmanuel: God with us. Which aspects of Christmas are easy to believe for you? Which parts do you struggle to believe?

 PRAY: Take a moment to praise God for revealing His sovereignty and power in the Christmas miracles. Ask Him to increase your faith in areas where you still struggle to believe.

Day 3
ISAAC: PREPARING FOR SURPRISES

READ: *Genesis 21:1–5, Genesis 22:1–14*

As children, we enjoyed opening presents on Christmas morning, anticipating great surprises. Some gifts were unexpected and brought us more joy than we could have imagined. Even the gifts we hoped for didn't fail to surprise us when we finally held them in our hands.

If we take a close look at the story of Jesus' arrival, we find that Christmas has always been full of exciting surprises: from Mary's miraculous conception to the sudden trip to Bethlehem, from a king born of peasants in a dirty stable to his birth announced to lowly shepherds.

Isaac's story prepares us to expect surprises, starting with his birth when his parents were well into their elderly years. But consider the range of surprises that Isaac experienced when he was alone on the mountain with Abraham.

Isaac pondered out loud the absence of a sacrificial lamb. And surely the answer must have taken him by surprise when Abraham bound him. But God wasn't done with surprises. Right at Isaac's most hopeless moment, as he was about to become the sacrifice, God surprised him with a ram to take his place. What joy Isaac must have known in that moment, having been given an unexpected gift that he would no doubt cherish for the rest of his life.

REFLECT: Think about some of the ways that Jesus has surprised you. Were you led to Jesus through an unexpected event? Have you experienced healing, or perhaps unexpected opportunities to help others? Have these moments prepared you to expect more surprises?

 PRAY: Take a moment to thank God for the unexpected grace He has shown you. Ask Him to prepare you to respond and act when He brings new surprises.

Day 4

JACOB: PREPARING FOR DISRUPTION

READ: *Genesis 25:21–34, Genesis 27:1–4, 32–45*

We put a lot of planning into Christmas, and sometimes our plans are disrupted. A winter storm or an illness may postpone or cancel a family gathering—despite our best planning.

We encounter disruption throughout the Christmas story, too. Jesus' anticipated arrival disrupted Joseph and Mary's plans to live the lives of Galilean commoners. The announcement of Jesus' birth drove Herod to disrupt the lives of countless families by ordering the death of all of the baby boys in the land.

Jacob's story is a series of disruptions that point us to the life and work of Jesus. First Jacob upended the cultural norms associated with birth order. When Esau relinquished his birthright to Jacob, his future was irrevocably disrupted. Esau's inheritance and stature now belonged to Jacob.

More disruption came when Esau sought his father's blessing and prepared to receive it. But his plans went awry when Jacob executed his own plan to claim Isaac's blessing for himself. And once the disruption happened, it couldn't be undone.

Yet, Jacob himself was not immune from disruption. Despite succeeding in his plans to swindle Esau of both his birthright and his father's blessing, Jacob had no time to enjoy the fruits of his deception. The threat against his life forced Jacob to flee, setting him on a new course from that point forward.

REFLECT: Can you think of a time when your plans came completely undone? Perhaps a promising job or an engagement fell through. Afterward, did you find new open doors that would not be possible any other way? What is unexpected to us is never a surprise to God.

 PRAY: Take time to thank God for the ways that He has seen you through unexpected times. If you are in the midst of disruption now, ask Him for guidance and wisdom.

Day 5

JACOB: PREPARING TO STRUGGLE

READ: *Genesis 32:1–6, 22–32*

Christmas is a difficult time for many. If you aren't struggling with the season, someone close to you probably is. Seasonal depression, financial strain, and broken relationships all have their weight amplified by the Christmas season.

In the Christmas story, we see that Jesus was born into struggle. His parents were young and poor. They had to endure a difficult trip to Bethlehem under the veiled threat of the Roman Empire. And when they arrived, they struggled to find lodging for themselves and bedding for the newborn Jesus.

Jacob's story prepares us to endure struggles. He had already fled his uncle in fear and was preparing to meet his estranged brother. Jacob felt the weight of pressure both behind him and ahead of him. In the midst of this struggle, he met a man who struggled with him to exhaustion.

Even as they wrestled, Jacob maintained enough hope to seek a blessing. And the blessing came, even as Jacob found himself unable to continue. When Jacob felt the full weight of his life and choices bearing down on him, he found that God had joined him in his struggle. Jacob's perspective was changed forever by the full realization of his encounter with God and the blessing that emerged from his struggle.

REFLECT: Think about seasons of difficulty that you've endured. Perhaps you're in such a season now. How did God show himself to you in those times? How does His presence in past difficulty change how you approach your present struggle or prepare for the next one?

 PRAY: Thank God for the ways that He has carried you through difficult seasons. If you're feeling weighed down now, invite Him to join your struggle and bear your burdens for you.

Day 6

JUDAH AND TAMAR: PREPARING TO DEAL WITH OUR MESS

READ: *Genesis 38:1–30*

We often take an idyllic view of the Christmas story: singing angels, serene shepherds, peaceful animals, and at the center of it all, smiling parents admiring their sleeping newborn. But the reality of Christmas is far messier: fearsome angels, gritty shepherds, smelly animals, and overwhelmed parents. And at the center of it all is Emmanuel—God with us, born into our mess, on purpose and with a purpose.

Fear, laced with superstition, had kept Judah from fulfilling his promise to Tamar after Judah's two oldest sons had died. Judah tried his best to ignore his failed promise by sending Tamar back to her father. Judah simply wasn't going to deal with this mess. Meanwhile, Tamar was stuck with the life of a widow—one that promised poverty and misery.

Having made a mess for Tamar, Judah then created a mess for himself when he sought out a prostitute to satisfy his own weakness. Instead he found Tamar, and she became pregnant by him. Of course, Tamar was prepared to reveal the truth at the right time.

Judah was humbled when his sin was exposed. The mess he had made was brought to light, and he could ignore it no further. So, Judah confessed his sin and restored Tamar to her promised place in his household, along with their twin sons.

REFLECT: Have you ever tried covering up or ignoring your sins and mistakes? Sooner or later, our messes grow too big to conceal. But when we confess our sins and deal with our messes in truth, we find Jesus addresses our mess, offering forgiveness and showing the way to restoration.

 PRAY: Take time to thank Jesus for stepping into your mess and forgiving your sins. Ask Him to reveal any unconfessed messes in your life and to guide you in wisdom to deal with them.

Day 7

NAHSHON, SON OF AMMINADAB: PREPARING TO GIVE

READ: *Numbers 7:10–17*

Many of us look forward to Christmas because we love to give. We enjoy the challenge of finding the perfect gifts, and we delight in seeing our gifts joyfully received by others. Charities ramp up their requests for donations as we get deeper into the season of giving, and we gladly respond!

While Jesus was still a small child in Bethlehem, Magi from the East brought him gifts fit for a king: gold, incense, and myrrh. During Jesus' ministry, he taught us to give freely, instructing us to provide food, drink, and clothing to the needy. He promised us that our heavenly Father, the greatest Giver of all, would provide all that we need.

Nahshon, son of Amminadab, had a special opportunity to give. When the tabernacle, the tent of worship, was completed, the leaders of Israel brought their offerings for its dedication. Nahshon was the first to give, presenting silver, gold, incense, grain, and meat. For each of the next 11 days, other leaders followed his example.

God used the gifts of His people to carry out His work then, and He does the same now. Whether we are giving to our local churches or meeting the needs of the poor and hungry, our gifts honor God and advance His kingdom.

REFLECT: Are you a carefree giver or a cautious giver? Are you more apt to give to your family and friends or to strangers in need? God is generous, and He invites us to share in His giving heart. How is He asking you to reflect His generosity?

 PRAY: Spend time thanking God for all that He has given you. Make a list and be specific. As you do, ask Him to show you an opportunity to give in a new way.

Day 8

RAHAB: PREPARING FOR A NEW WAY OF LIFE

READ: *Joshua 2:1–16, Joshua 6:15–17, 22–25*

Christmastime often stirs up the idea of making changes. For some, the approaching new year inspires resolutions. For others, the time with family and the spirit of giving cause us to reexamine our time and our priorities. Some of us make small, incremental changes. Others embark on a whole new way of life.

Jesus' arrival sparked a new way of life for many people. During his infancy, his parents were forced to live as refugees in Egypt. And during Jesus' ministry, fisherman, tax collectors, and others left behind their trades and their lifestyles to follow him.

Rahab's story also marks a life-altering turning point. The people of Jericho were awash with fear as the Israelites approached their city. When Israel's spies arrived, Rahab saw an opportunity to leave behind the ways of Jericho and embrace a new way of life. She saw that the Israelites were sent by God, and in that she saw an opportunity to be rescued from her fear—and perhaps even from her life as a prostitute.

The New Testament writers hold Rahab up as an example of faith because she trusted in God's deliverance. And God faithfully spared Rahab and her family, as her city—in fact her entire way of life—was burned away. In its place, Rahab found a new family and a new direction with a new purpose.

REFLECT: Think of the big changes that you've made in your life. What prompted them? Maybe you're right where God wants you to be. But on the other hand, maybe He is prompting a change. Is He speaking to you through a current crisis or a pending opportunity?

 PRAY: Thank God for leading you through the changes—both great and small—that you've experienced. Ask Him to reveal any new direction He may be calling you to and to prepare you for what comes next.

Day 9
RUTH: PREPARING FOR ADOPTION

READ: *Ruth 1:1–22*

For many of us, the Christmas season is a time to return home. Even if we've built our own lives in new cities and new surroundings, home might be grandma's house or perhaps a childhood church. But for some of us, home is elusive: It's wherever we are at that moment. Or it's nowhere at all.

When Jesus was a child, home eluded him, too. From his birth in Bethlehem to his flight to Egypt, it would take some time before he made his way to a home in Nazareth. In his ministry, he promised to prepare his disciples a heavenly home. And as our savior, his love made a way for us to be adopted as sons and daughters of God.

Ruth, a Moabite woman, also found herself longing for a home and a family. Her husband, an Israelite from the tribe of Judah, had died and left her widowed at a young age. She could have chosen to start over among her people.

But she had experienced, however briefly, what it meant to be a part of the family of God's people. And so she chose to remain with Naomi, with Israel, and with God. Even with no husband and an uncertain future, Ruth had a family and an identity with God and His people.

REFLECT: We all have vastly different family experiences. Whether your family was large or small, affectionate or distant, how do you relate to Ruth's story? As a child adopted by God, how do you relate to the Father and to your brothers and sisters in Christ?

 PRAY: Thank God, our Father Abba, for making you his child. Thank Him for His care, for His love, and for the eternal home He provides. Ask Him to make you resemble Him more each day.

Day 10

BOAZ: PREPARING FOR REDEMPTION

READ: *Ruth 2:1–3, 3:1–13, 4:1–10*

In our modern usage, the idea of redemption is small and transactional. For example, when we shop for Christmas gifts, we redeem coupons and discount codes for special deals. Perhaps we've saved our loyal shopper points to redeem them for a ham at the grocery store.

When we read the story of Boaz, we see redemption as something much bigger. Yes, there was a transaction involved when Boaz purchased a field from Naomi. But unlike our transactions, which might result in getting better quality merchandise, Boaz's redemptive act was life changing—both for him and for Ruth.

Without Boaz's intervention, Naomi and Ruth would have been left to poverty with no hope of a secure future. Boaz showed them compassion through his act of redemption because he saw that Ruth was worth redeeming, and he was willing to pay the price. He wasn't after the field, but he purchased it to ensure that Ruth could be redeemed.

When the angel first visited Joseph, he told him that Jesus will save us from our sins—that he would redeem us. Like Ruth, we needed intervention. And like Boaz, Jesus paid a great price because of his desire to redeem you and me. Jesus came to pay the price, as well as to be the price for our rescue.

REFLECT: Have you ever considered how much Jesus values you? The price of your redemption was costly, and God knew that neither you nor anybody else could ever pay it. So, He redeemed you by sending Jesus to pay his own life to purchase yours.

 PRAY: Thank God for sending Jesus to pay for your sins and purchase your eternal security. Contemplate the depth of His love for you that He would pay such a price to win you to Himself.

Day 11

JESSE: PREPARING TO RETHINK OUR PRIORITIES

READ: *1 Samuel 16:1–13*

As children, we approached Christmas with a focus on our wants. But we had to endure tedious church services, long car trips, and visits with distant relatives before we could get to the presents. When we received our gifts, if they let us down, our parents would tell us, "It's the thought that counts."

Most of us outgrew our selfish priorities. We began to appreciate time with the family, and church became meaningful. Maybe this change had something to do with the King born to a peasant and made to sleep in a manger because he had—as we sing each year—no crib for a bed.

The anointing of Israel's second king reminds us that Jesus' humble beginnings weren't new. When the Lord sent the prophet Samuel to anoint one of Jesse's sons as the next king, Jesse had a picture in mind of what made a good king, so he presented his tallest and finest son. But God had other ideas.

In all, Jesse presented seven sons to Samuel without even considering David. After all, Jesse thought that David was too young and too small. He was better suited to the pasture than the throne or the battlefield. It wasn't until Samuel pressed him that Jesse could see past his own ideals and consider that God's priorities were not the same as his own.

REFLECT: How has God reshaped your priorities over the years? Has losing family members drawn you closer to the ones that are still with you? Have you endured seasons of financial difficulty that turned your focus away from material excess? Does your current attitude toward others reflect these changes?

 PRAY: Is there someone in your life who you've dismissed as too difficult or too useless? Ask God to show you how He sees that person and how you can approach them with fresh eyes.

Day 12

DAVID: PREPARING TO REVEAL GOD'S GLORY

READ: *1 Samuel 17:1–11, 32–40, 48–58*

Many people anticipate Christmas with great fanfare. It is a time of year when we enjoy extravagant decorating. Some cities gather at a Christmas tree in the center of town, and some families drive around the neighborhood to check out the light shows. More than a few of us look forward to seeing how the White House tree turns out.

Yet, Jesus' birth was not anticipated by any fanfare at all. He was born to peasants, and his arrival was announced to lowly shepherds. There was no parade, nor calling together of the townspeople—just some angels singing, "Glory to God in the Highest."

Perhaps there is no better reminder that all glory belongs to God than the story of David and Goliath. Goliath was an accomplished warrior, who was celebrated and glorified by the Philistines. Not one soldier among Israel's men was willing to face him. They all saw measuring up to Goliath's greatness as an impossible task.

David wasn't even a warrior, yet he knew that God's glory was greater than Goliath's. The king's armor was not a fit for David, so he went into battle without the royal crest. Unadorned and meagerly armed, David trusted God to do the impossible. Yet despite his victory, David was so unassuming that even King Saul had no idea who he was.

REFLECT: In what ways do the hype and celebration of the Christmas season draw your attention away from God's glory? Do you seek out—and draw attention to—grand displays and prominent people? How does David's victory over Goliath help you to redirect your attention and praise to God?

 PRAY: Take some time to reflect on God's glory. He created the stars, and He sent the angelic choir to sing His glory. No human display or celebration can match His greatness.

Day 13

DAVID AND BATHSHEBA: PREPARING FOR CONVICTION

READ: *2 Samuel 11:1–17, 26–27 12:1–13*

As children, we were often reminded by our parents and our own conscience of the importance of making sure our names were on Santa's nice list and staying off of his naughty list. We didn't want to suffer the consequence of having our Christmas gifts replaced with coal.

As adults, whether we dismiss Santa's lists as silly or we use them to manage our own children, we've grown to understand that actions have consequences.

John describes Jesus as a light coming into the darkness. Darkness hides from the light, and we might try to keep our own sins hidden in the dark. But sin and its consequences ultimately catch up with us, and Jesus has come to do something about it.

No story highlights our need for rescue from our own sins better than the story of David and Bathsheba. David stepped into sin with his first indiscretion with Bathsheba, and he further compounded his sin by trying to cover up each past sin with a new sin, hiding them in the darkness.

It wasn't until the prophet Nathan shined the light of truth on David that he was able to turn to the Lord in repentance and receive the rescue that eluded him. David couldn't erase his sins. He needed divine light to dispel the darkness.

REFLECT: We often meditate on repentance during Lent, not Advent. But Easter is the reason that we celebrate Christmas because Jesus was born to rescue us from sin and death. As you welcome the light of Jesus anew this Christmas, consider: Are there areas of your life that remain in darkness?

 PRAY: Confess to Jesus those sins that still hide in the dark places of your heart and mind. Ask Him to shine the light of His grace on your life to dispel the darkness as you repent and receive His forgiveness.

Day 14

SOLOMON: PREPARING TO SEEK WISDOM

READ: *1 Kings 3:1–15*

As you've browsed store Christmas displays and scrolled through social media, you've no doubt encountered the phrase "Wise men still seek Him," accompanied by images of magi on camelback following a star to find Jesus.

Have you ever thought about why we call the Magi "wise men"? Were they wise because they were educated? Because they recognized that Jesus was worthy of worship? Or because they were compelled to seek him out? Where does wisdom come from?

When we think of wisdom, many of us are reminded of Solomon. His wisdom is preserved in the proverbs and other writings, and some of his sayings have even spread beyond the church and into common use in society. Much of Solomon's reign was marked by peace and sound judgment. Rulers form neighboring nations sought his counsel.

Yet Solomon was not wise because of his own standing or education. He was wise because he sought wisdom from the Lord. He could have asked the Lord for anything. He could have been shortsighted and self-serving in his requests. When he asked the Lord for a discerning heart, the Lord responded with gladness.

Perhaps it takes a little wisdom to know to seek more wisdom. But to all who ask for wisdom, God promises to grant it generously.

REFLECT: How much does wisdom drive your decisions? As you look back on the year that is wrapping up and plan for the year ahead, in what ways are you seeking wisdom? Do prayer, research, and input from your spouse or your trusted friends factor into your planning?

 PRAY: Thank God for His generous outpouring of wisdom. Bring Him your worries, plans, and hopes and ask Him to guide your decisions by His wisdom. Ask Him to surround you with wise counsel in the year ahead.

Day 15
REHOBOAM: PREPARING TO BE HUMBLED

READ: *2 Chronicles 10:1–17, 12:1–12*

Many families have fun giving gifts under the guise of the Santa Claus tale. But Santa brings unintended consequences to our culture. Specifically, Santa conditions us to build up our expectations in unhealthy and self-serving ways.

But Jesus' arrival subverts our cultural expectations. Jesus' genealogy, as recorded in Matthew, reveals that Joseph should have been the king of Israel. But through a series of historic events, the royal succession of David's line had been disrupted, and instead Jesus was born to a poor Nazorean family. Why?

Because God's kingdom is a culture of humility, not loftiness. So, the kings needed to be humbled in a big way. And no king reflects this need better than Rehoboam.

Under Solomon's reign, the royal family accumulated great wealth and prestige. But the workers were weary, and when Rehoboam succeeded his father as king, they sought relief. In response, Rehoboam promised to increase their burden. So, the people abandoned him, leaving him with only the regions of Judah and Benjamin under his rule.

Foreign rulers took advantage of Rehoboam's vulnerability, and his territory was overtaken. It wasn't until he was faced with the loss of his people and his possessions that Rehoboam returned to the Lord—humbled.

REFLECT: To some degree, all of us place expectations on ourselves and others. Take some time to consider the basis for your expectations. Are they rooted in your job title or your prominence in the community? Or do you base your expectations on God's kingdom values of humility and kindness?

 PRAY: Ask God to reveal where and how you can practice greater humility. Let Him show you ways that you can serve others, so that He may be lifted up through your work.

Day 16

ABIJAH: PREPARING FOR UNDESERVED FAVOR

READ: *1 Kings 15:1–4, 2 Chronicles 13:4–20*

Have you ever received a gift that was so valuable or so significant that your first reaction was to think, "I don't deserve this"? How did your reaction affect how you viewed the giver, yourself, and your relationship? Did you puzzle over how you could have possibly earned the gift, or did you simply respond with gratitude?

When the angel Gabriel announced Jesus' pending arrival to Mary, he twice told her that she was favored. He didn't say why, and Mary was more than a little confused. Yet, she didn't ask what she did to earn such a special honor. Instead, she accepted God's will and purpose for her life with gratitude and a servant's heart.

Abijah's reign over Judah was short, lasting only three years, and like his father, Rehoboam, his heart was not devoted to the Lord. Yet, God saw fit to grant Abijah a victory that had been denied his father: the defeat of Jeroboam, king of Israel. Why? For the sake of His covenant with David.

God's plan was bigger than one person. God blessed Abijah's reign with an increase in his territory, so that through Abijah, His will could be done, His covenant preserved, and His plan carried out.

REFLECT: How much of what you've been given was earned, and how much was freely given? How does Jesus' generosity affect how you give to others? Do you share your kindness with the most deserving people, or do you share it with all of the people who God places in your life?

 PRAY: Take some time to thank God for His grace, for the free gift of salvation and the undeserved pardon that Jesus purchased for you. Ask Him to show you how you can live as a testimony to His grace in your life.

Day 17
ASA: PREPARING TO RELY ON GOD

READ: *2 Chronicles 14:2–12, 16:1–13*

Christmas is a busy time of year. Whether you're ordering gifts, coordinating an office party, or assigning side dishes for the family dinner, you expect that everyone else will do their part to turn plans into results. But sometimes, people let us down. Even in the little disappointments, we are reminded of how much we rely on God.

Mary and Joseph had to rely on God during the first Christmas. They traveled to Bethlehem assuming that they could rely on someone to give them shelter, but they were out of traditional options. Yet, God saved them a spot in a stable. It wasn't ideal by our standards, but it was perfect for reminding us of our reliance on God.

King Asa's story in *2 Chronicles* also reminds us how much we need to rely on God. When he turned to the Lord for help against the approaching Cushite army in chapter 14, the Lord provided a swift victory. But later, he forgot the Lord and relied on human alliances, even giving wealth from the Temple treasury to the king of Aram.

Hanani the seer pointed out Asa's foolishness and warned him that his remaining days would be filled with conflict. Asa did not react kindly, and had Hanani thrown in prison. Even illness couldn't persuade Asa to remember the 35 years of peace he enjoyed when he relied on the Lord.

REFLECT: King Asa's story doesn't have a happy ending, but your story isn't over. Are you relying on God or on human allies, particularly in your professional life? If you've shut God out of an area of your life, what would change if you placed your reliance on Him?

 PRAY: Take time to thank God for all of the ways that He has provided for you. Ask Him to reveal any areas where you rely on other people instead of Him and commit to relying on Him more fully.

Day 18

JEHOSHAPHAT: PREPARING TO SEEK THE LORD'S COUNSEL

READ: *1 Kings 22:41–44, 2 Chronicles 18:1–19, 20:1–4*

Even amidst the busy pace of the Christmas season, many of us are looking ahead to the new year. We plan, we prepare, and we resolve. But when we're faced with the big decisions that have life-altering impact, where do we turn for advice? It's easy to make up our minds and seek out opinions that validate our perspective, but that doesn't always lead us to truth or to God's will.

Jesus arrived as a light in the darkness. His light challenges the world's darkness, and sometimes it is uncomfortable, but it is always revealing. The story of Jehoshaphat reminds us of this contrast, and it reminds us of the benefit of living in Jesus' light.

Jehoshaphat made a habit of seeking Godly counsel, and the Lord faithfully answered him. Even when Ahab, king of Israel, turned to his people-pleasing false prophets for counsel, Jehoshaphat urged him to consider the voice of one lone prophet who was willing to speak God's truth.

The result was revealing indeed, foretelling Ahab's defeat and shining the bright light of truth on his foolish refusal to seek, much less hear, the voice of God. By contrast, Jehoshaphat continued to seek God, heed His directives, and witness the hand of God at work in his reign.

REFLECT: How do you react when God's wisdom clashes with your own? Do you avoid aspects of God's Word that challenge your political ideals or your personal ambitions? What part of your life is most in need of the revealing light of Christ?

 PRAY: If you're facing big decisions, ask God to guide your thought process. Ask Him to reveal His purpose for your life and to lead you to a wise pastor or Godly friend to help you see your choices by the light of Christ so that you may walk more closely with Him.

Day 19
JEHORAM: PREPARING FOR ACCOUNTABILITY

READ: *2 Chronicles 21:4–20*

As we approach the end of the year, many of us look back and assess what we have accomplished. For some people, this process might be formalized with a performance review at work. For others, it might include an examination our previous New Year's resolutions. For all, failure to perform as expected might result in consequences.

Likewise, if we are accustomed to buying extravagant gifts and hosting Christmas celebrations, our bank statements and credit card bills will reveal next month whether we adhered to our budgets or got reckless with our spending. If we weren't careful, the bill will reveal the magnitude of our consequences.

Accountability is a part of life. Perhaps no story reminds us of the reality of accountability more than the story of Jehoram, who made a conscious choice to turn from God, kill his brothers, and lead the people astray through the worship of false gods. God swiftly held Jehoram to account, relieving him of his family, wealth, and health. Jehoram's reign was short and miserable, and his death was not mourned.

But even while holding Jehoram to account, God preserved his lineage for the sake of His covenant. By a strand of grace, God left Jehoram an heir, a bit of hope that would bring us a step closer to Jesus and his fulfillment of God's plan.

REFLECT: As Jesus grows us in grace, He holds us accountable for how we use His grace. In *Matthew 25*, the parable of the talents reminds us that we play a part in passing on His grace. Does God's grace compel you to worship, to care for the needs of others, and to pass on God's grace to those around you?

 PRAY: Thank God for His saving and sustaining grace. Ask Him to show you where you can pass that grace on to others. Is there someone who He is calling you to help, encourage, or witness to?

Day 20

UZZIAH AND JOTHAM: PREPARING TO CONFRONT OUR PRIDE

READ: *2 Chronicles 26:3–8, 16–21, 27:1–4, 6*

It is satisfying to watch our children open their gifts on Christmas morning with delight on their faces. And it is easy to feel a sense of accomplishment, or even pride, at such a small success.

Perhaps, it's too easy.

Pride has a way of creeping in to even the simplest and noblest of our actions. In Jesus' sermon on the mount, he warned that when we give for the sake of being recognized, recognition from men is the most reward that we can expect. But when we give out of compassion, without any thought of reward, we do the Father's work.

King Uzziah shows us how such misplaced pride can be our downfall. The Lord had built Uzziah up as a successful, powerful king. But Uzziah let his success become a source of pride. In his pride, he thought he was fit to burn incense in the temple. But when he failed to heed the warning of the priests, God brought an end to his success.

From Uzziah's isolation, he could only watch as his son Jotham took over his reign. And though details of Jotham's story are sparse and have been lost to history, he honored God with his actions. During Jotham's reign, God's brought growth and renewal to the temple and the towns of Judea.

REFLECT: What motivates your good deeds? Whether you are providing bonuses to your employees, gifts to your children, or donations to the needy, are you seeking recognition or only the joy of doing God's work? How can you guard against the pride that brought Uzziah's downfall?

 PRAY: Take time to thank God for the good that He has done for you and through you. Praise Him for His kindness and grace. Ask Him to lead you to opportunities to reveal His glory through your actions.

Day 21

AHAZ: PREPARING TO CONFRONT OUR IDOLS

READ: *2 Kings 16:1–18, 2 Chronicles 28:1–5, 22–25*

If you've been watching TV in recent weeks, you've probably grown tired of commercials. Every year, we're encouraged to chase after the latest smartphone and surprise our spouse with a new luxury car. The message is simple: Nice things will make us happy, and they will show our neighbors that we are important and special. There is no shortage of idols available to us in our culture.

The Christmas story challenges our idols. God didn't choose kings, palaces, and comfort to usher in Jesus' birth. Instead, he chose an impoverished couple, lowly shepherds, and a stable, far away from the idols of wealth and prestige.

No king in Jesus' family tree reveals the dangers of idolatry better than King Ahaz. The Bible tells us that Ahaz turned from God, even sacrificing his sons to fire in his selfish pursuits. But why?

Ahaz desired the status and prestige enjoyed by surrounding nations. He sought dangerous alliances and adopted the idol worship of neighboring kingdoms, all for the sake of attaining security and favor. He gave up the Lord's treasures, and he was left subservient to the king of Aram.

In addition, Ahaz set up altars to false gods on every street corner in every town. But peace eluded him, and his idols ended up controlling him instead of bringing him joy.

REFLECT: Do you find peace and contentment in Jesus, or do you experience a restless desire to increase your wealth, improve your status, or impress your neighbors? How does the story of Ahaz help you to guard against putting your hope in earthly possessions and prestige?

 PRAY: Acknowledge that all good things come from God and that the gift can never be greater than the Giver. Invite Him to turn your heart away from the things that compete with Him for your attention and affection.

Day 22

HEZEKIAH: PREPARING TO WORSHIP IN TRUTH

READ: *2 Kings 18:1–8, 17–25, 19:14–19, 20:1–6*

The Christmas season brings music that we don't hear any other time of year. We gather in our churches and proclaim Joy to the World. And we put our all into holding the "Glo-o-o-oria" of "Angels We Have Heard on High."

At the first Christmas, the praise songs of the angels encouraged the shepherds to worship. Their songs still encourage our worship today. Like the angels and shepherds, King Hezekiah was motivated by his desire to worship God.

Hezekiah had previously witnessed the idolatry of his father, Ahaz. Just a few years into his own reign, Hezekiah saw the northern kingdom of Israel fall to the Assyrians, who were quick to bring in their own false gods. Only Judah remained, and Hezekiah's first objective was to return Judah to proper worship of the One True God.

Hezekiah removed the altars that had been set up by his father, confusing his enemies. They wondered, "How could Hezekiah worship after removing all of the altars?" But Hezekiah knew that he was not seeking after the false gods of his father, but the One God who was worthy of praise.

When trouble reached his doorstep, Hezekiah had the confidence to trust in the Lord. God answered Hezekiah's desire to know Him by revealing Himself and providing deliverance to Judah.

REFLECT: Culture and history sometimes provide us a distorted understanding of God. But to worship in truth, we must seek God as He really is. When you seek God, do you rely on preconceived expectations and ideas, or do you seek to know God as He is revealed in scripture?

 PRAY: Turn to God with an open heart and mind. Ask Him to fill you with His Spirit and illuminate His Word so that as you read, you may know Him more fully.

Day 23

MANASSEH: PREPARING FOR REDIRECTION

READ: *2 Chronicles 33:1–17*

The angels announced the arrival of a savior. John described Jesus' arrival as light entering the darkness. These proclamations tell us that Jesus has come to change the hearts and trajectory of all who receive him.

Change of heart is a common theme of our favorite Christmas stories. Every year, we enjoy watching George Bailey, Ebenezer Scrooge, and even the Grinch experience profound encounters that set them on a new path with changed hearts.

Like the characters in these tales, Manasseh was the obvious villain of his story. He rebuilt the altars to false gods, and he also practiced divination, astrology, and even child sacrifice.

Manasseh ignored the prophets that the Lord sent to him. It would take a profound encounter to change him.

Manasseh's encounter came when he was captured by the Assyrian king. Shackled and fitted with a nose ring, Manasseh was humbled and defeated. But God did not allow the story to end there. He heard Manasseh's plea and restored him to his throne—changed and renewed.

Much like we see in our TV movies, Manasseh's story ends with him righting wrongs and turning from evil as he led the people of Judah to return to the Lord.

REFLECT: Think about how far Jesus has brought you from where he first found you. If you are struggling with the areas of your heart and life that still need to change, how does Manasseh's story give you hope that God will complete His good work in you?

 PRAY: Thank God for rescuing you from your sin and turning you away from destruction. Ask Him to reveal the areas of your heart that still need to change as you surrender to the transforming power of His grace.

Day 24

JOSIAH, SON OF AMON: PREPARING FOR RENEWAL

READ: *2 Chronicles 33:21–25, 34:1–3, 8–9, 14–32*

One of the appeals of Christmas is that we get to know Jesus as an infant. We get to take a moment and remember that the great teacher, leader, and messiah who we love came to us as a baby—Emmanuel, God with us.

Maybe our fondness for Jesus' infancy has something to do with the joy we experience whenever we hear stories about children doing wonderful things. New stories pop up every year about children collecting coats for the homeless, buying toys for needy children, or performing other acts of compassion. These stories often give us hope and encouragement, renewing our own desire to serve others with compassion.

So, we are especially encouraged by the story of Josiah, who became king at age eight after an assassin cut his father's reign short. Even in Josiah's youth, he sought the Lord and was determined to right the wrongs of his recent predecessors.

Josiah's passion for renewal led him to repair the temple, and he ultimately led his people in restoring their long-forgotten covenant with the Lord. Of course, by then Josiah was no longer a boy, but a young man. Still, the renewal that King Josiah encouraged and led all started with a young boy's desire to seek God and his determination to see worship restored.

REFLECT: If you have children, have you observed their sometimes idealistic hopes and goals? As a parent, older sibling, or church leader, how can you learn from that childlike passion and encourage the children in your life to put their faith and compassion into action?

 PRAY: Thank God for the children he has placed in your life. Ask Him to show you how you can learn from them and be encouraged and renewed in your own faith journey.

Day 25

JECONIAH: PREPARING FOR A CHANGE OF PLANS

READ: *2 Kings 24:8–17*

We put a lot of effort into planning around Christmastime. We have family gatherings, social obligations, and church services that all need to be aligned and coordinated. The slightest disruption can set off a chain reaction that completely changes our plans.

Mary and Joseph were no strangers to a sudden change of plans. They had received unexpected news about Jesus' arrival, and they also had to make an unplanned trip to Bethlehem at the height of Mary's pregnancy. Certainly, if Mary and Joseph had been in control of their plans, they would have done things quite differently.

But perhaps the disruption brought on by a change of plans is best seen in the story of King Jeconiah. Taking over the throne when he was only 18 years old, Jeconiah (called Jehoiachin in the Old Testament) no doubt had his own ambitions and agenda. He likely looked forward to a long reign of carrying out those plans.

But Jeconiah never had the chance to put his plans into action. Having been captured and exiled only three months into his reign, he was quickly stripped of his crown and replaced by his uncle. Whatever aspirations Jeconiah had were now out of reach. From this point forward, God had a new plan for the line of David, the people of Judah, and ultimately all of humanity.

REFLECT: Have you ever been frustrated by a disruption in your plans? What was the outcome? Did you experience results that would not have been possible under your original plan? Sometimes, God disrupts our plans when the old way isn't working, and He is working out something new for us.

 PRAY: Praise God for His sovereignty. Thank Him for being at work in your situation before you even know your needs. Ask Him to light your steps each day so you can walk according to His plan for you.

Day 26

ZERUBBABEL SON OF SHEALTIEL: PREPARING FOR HOPE

READ: *Ezra 3:1–11, Haggai 2:1–9*

As children, we often looked forward to Christmas with great anticipation. On Christmas Eve, our parents struggled to get us to sleep because we were so filled with expectation and hope for the day ahead.

Hope is threaded throughout the angels' announcement to the shepherds. "We have good news that will bring great joy," they declared. The arrival of the savior, they tell us, means a better future. He is the embodiment of hope.

Hope is at the center of Zerubbabel's story. His grandfather had been stripped of his crown and carried off into exile along with the rest of the people of Judah. Jerusalem and the temple had been destroyed and remained in ruins for 70 years.

When the time had come for the people to return and rebuild, Zerubbabel led the rebuilding of the temple. He worked with the hope that God's glory would be restored, and he also hoped that the new temple would glorify God even more than the first!

Zerubbabel was so sure of his hope that even before the foundation of the temple was laid, he rebuilt the altar so the people could once again worship the Lord. Even though construction had barely begun, Zerubbabel led the people to look ahead to the future glory of the new temple through the eyes of hope.

REFLECT: Does childlike hope come easily to you, or have the pressures and challenges of adult life left you jaded? How does Zerubbabel's determination in the midst of ruin help you to find hope in God, in His plan, and in the work that He continues to do in you?

 PRAY: Thank God for the hope that He gives you through Jesus. Ask Him to take hold of your doubts and guide you through your current difficulties. Rest in the assurance that God is present in all circumstances.

Day 27
JOSEPH: PREPARING TO TRUST GOD

READ: *Matthew 1:18–25, 2:13–23*

Sometimes Christmas doesn't meet our expectations. Failed promises from family members or difficulty finding the right gifts might leave us disappointed. Some of us are so accustomed to disappointment that we expect bad outcomes, not only on Christmas but throughout life.

So, we try to engineer perfect solutions to our problems. We try to make everything as right as possible through our own efforts. And we still end up disappointed.

In these times, maybe God is revealing a solution that doesn't seem to make sense but is perfectly designed by Him to work.

This is the situation that Joseph found himself in. Mary was pregnant, and that looked bad for Joseph's marriage and for his future. It seemed to him that a trust had been broken. It took a messenger in a dream to change Joseph's perspective, to convince Joseph to put away his fear and doubt and trust what God was doing, no matter how bad he thought it looked.

Joseph trusted, and he later witnessed the glorious arrival of Jesus. And when it came time to trust God again and take his family to Egypt, we read no doubt in Joseph's response as he listened and obeyed the God who had already shown Himself to be trustworthy.

REFLECT: You probably live a normal life. But what do you do when normal doesn't work? Or how about when normal works just fine, but God is leading you to something different? Does doubt motivate your response, or do you trust God even when it doesn't seem to make sense?

 PRAY: Thank God for the times that He has shown His faithfulness to you. Commit to trusting Him more. If there are areas of your life where you have resisted God's direction, surrender those areas to Him.

Day 28
MARY: PREPARING TO SERVE GOD

READ: *Luke 1:26–38, 46–50*

Christmas is a time of year that prompts many of us to serve others. The cultural emphasis on gift giving, the desire to connect with family, and the onset of winter temperatures each, in their own way, bring the needy to mind and compel us to take action.

Mary was the first person to hear the good news of Jesus' pending arrival. And she responded with a willingness to serve. She may not have understood how Jesus' miraculous arrival came to be. And she was perplexed that she, of all people, would be chosen to be his mother. But she was prepared to serve however God called her to serve.

Throughout Jesus' ministry and especially in his death, serving is a continuing theme. Jesus taught that he came to serve, rather than to be served. He instructs each of us to serve one another in love, just as he has faithfully served us. He calls us to turn our service outward to the communities around us. To the hungry and thirsty, the sick and imprisoned, the widows and orphans.

Sometimes, God calls us to uncomfortable places or to service that we don't fully understand. Such was the case with Mary, who answered the strange new call with five simple words: "I am the Lord's servant."

REFLECT: How do you use your time and talent to serve God and others? Does the Christmas season make it easier for you to serve? Service didn't stop with Mary, and it doesn't stop with Christmas. In what ways can you keep your attitude of service going throughout the year?

 PRAY: Thank God for all the ways that He faithfully serves you. Answer His grace with a commitment to pass on His grace to others. Ask Him to direct you to places where you can serve Him more.

ACKNOWLEDGMENTS

Thank you, first and foremost, to my God for calling me to new life in Jesus and being my reason for writing.

Thank you to my wife, Angela, for telling me that I was a writer before I even realized it, and for encouraging and supporting this new trajectory of my life in every way imaginable.

Thank you to my sons, Kyle and John Mark, for sharing my excitement and providing enthusiastic support to this project.

Thank you to my editor/publisher/navigator Jennifer for doing all of the things that I don't know how to do to turn a stack of words into an actual book.

And thank you to all of my friends and family who have, in your own unique ways, impacted my faith journey.

ABOUT THE AUTHOR

Jac Filer is a lifelong resident of Bucks County, Pennsylvania, where he presently lives with his family. Since 2020, he has been enjoying a second career as a freelance Christian writer and is an ongoing contributor to multiple blogs, web sites, and devotional apps. Preparing for Jesus is Jac's first book.

CPSIA information can be obtained
at www.ICGtesting.com
Printed in the USA
BVHW092032161122
652041BV00003B/15